# What Time Is It?

*Ralph Martin*

**SERVANT BOOKS**
Ann Arbor, Michigan

# What Time Is It?

TIME PLAYS AN IMPORTANT ROLE in our daily lives. When we look at our watch, we see that it is a certain hour. Perhaps our watch even indicates the date and the day of the week. Our watches tell us something useful. They help us to know when we should stop doing one thing and move on to another. They let us know how much time we have left to complete a particular task.

Our watches also tell us something useful for our spiritual lives, maybe something more useful than we might think. They tell us we only have a limited number of days, a limited number of hours to live our lives on this earth—this particular year, this particular day, this particular hour, are the only ones like this that we will ever experience. For that reason, how important it is that we accomplish God's purpose for this hour, day, date, and year!

## *God's Time*

Yet scripture tells us that God has his own way of measuring time, a way that we will never discover simply by looking at our watches. In 2 Peter 3:8, we learn that "in the Lord's eyes, one day is as a thousand years and a thousand years are as a day." God has another way of measuring time. We have to learn spiritual sensitivity to God's timetable in order to be in tune with his purposes.

What time is it in God's plan? Where are we in God's timetable? What is the significance of the time in which we are living? What is important and what is not so important? Scripture tells us some important things about God's time. First of all, it tells us that we are living in the last age: the time between the first and second comings of Jesus Christ. When God's Son appeared, the culmination of God's plan for the human race manifested itself and the last age of human history was ushered in.

This is also a time of mercy and forgiveness. In Hebrews 9:27-28 we read: "Just as it is appointed that men die once, and after death be judged, so Christ was offered up once to take away the sins of many; he will appear a second time not to take away sin but to bring salvation to those who eagerly await him." Here, St. Paul is telling us that in this age, God is offering us forgiveness in the person of his Son, Jesus Christ. This is the time to proclaim the Good News of Jesus Christ so that as many people as possible will turn to him, call upon his name, and be saved. Jesus Christ, who came the first time as a sacrificial lamb to take away the sins of the world, is coming again in glory as king and as judge to cleanse the universe of wickedness and to welcome into his Father's house all who have received and accepted the grace, mercy, and pardon he offers. We are living in the last age of human history. We are making the one choice that will determine whether our life is a success or not—to choose for Jesus Christ and to be faithful to him until the end.

Another important thing that scripture tells us about God's time is that God often has a timetable for working with a particular nation, city, individual, and with what scripture refers to as "generations." Scripture often relates how God deals with a certain group of people at a certain time in history, often in a certain place and in a certain way. These were times of visitation—moments when God dealt with a particular group of people in a special way. Their response to these visitations had concrete consequences. For example, the people of Nineveh repented and were saved. The people of Sodom and Gomorrah did not and were destroyed.

Consider the story of Abraham and his nephew Lot as related in Genesis 18 and 19. The evil in Sodom and Gomorrah was so great that God simply could not withhold his justice and judgment any longer; he determined that the time had come to destroy the cities.

Abraham was a friend of God. Because he was a

friend of God, God showed Abraham what he was about to do. Abraham had relatives in Sodom—his nephew Lot and his family—and he did not want his relatives to experience that judgment. He began to bargain with the Lord: "Suppose there were fifty innocent people in the city; would you wipe out the place, rather than spare it for the sake of the fifty innocent people within it?" The Lord replied, "If I find fifty innocent people in the city of Sodom, I will spare the whole place for their sake." Nevertheless, Abraham thought he might have set the figure too high, so he began to negotiate with the Lord. "What if there are five less than fifty innocent people? Will you destroy the whole city because of those five?" The Lord answered, "I will not destroy it . . . if I find forty-five there." Abraham thought the figure might still be too high. Time and again he went back to the Lord to ask if he would spare the city for the sake of forty, then thirty, then twenty, and finally ten innocent people. Each time the Lord said he was willing to spare the city for those innocent few. How much God was willing to do for the sake of his friend! How much God is willing to do today for the sake of his friends! (Gn 18:24-32)

When God sent his angels to the city of Sodom, it was obvious that there were not even ten innocent people in the city. In fact, the people of Sodom were so wicked they even tried to sexually abuse God's angels. But God was willing to spare Abraham's relatives, so the angels went to Lot's house and said, "Take everyone that belongs to you and immediately flee the city." Lot told his daughters and sons-in-law that they had to immediately leave the city, but his sons-in-law thought he was joking. Lot, his wife, and his daughters were willing to go but hesitated, so the angels grabbed them by the hand and led them to safety. Then fire fell upon Sodom and Gommorah—the fire of God's judgment.

The generation of Noah is yet another example of how God deals with a wicked generation when time runs out for that generation (Gn 6, 7). In the time of Noah, wickedness, corruption, perversion, and ungodliness had reached such a point that God could no longer withhold his judgment. He decided to wipe out that unrighteous generation from the face of the earth. Yet God intervened to save a faithful remnant. God told Noah to build an ark for himself and his family because a great flood was going to cover the earth. Noah spent a great deal of time building the ark, and his neighbors probably laughed at him—until the flood came. How important it is to follow the direction of the Lord, even in the face of ridicule and laughter! How important it is to understand what God is saying and to be ready for what will unfold!

In the time of Jonah, God decided that time had run out for Nineveh. But Nineveh was given one more chance; God commissioned Jonah to go into the city, walk across it, and tell the inhabitants to repent or face God's judgment. Jonah did not want to do what God commanded him to do, but he finally did it. Nineveh repented. The people took the chance God gave them, repented in sackcloth and ashes, and were saved.

In Luke 19:41-44 we read about another visitation that God made to his people—Jesus' visitation to the people of Jerusalem almost 2,000 years ago:

> Coming within sight of the city, he wept over it and said: "If only you had known the path to peace this day; but you have completely lost it from view! Days will come upon you when your enemies will encircle you with a rampart, hem you in, and press you hard from every side. They will wipe you out, you and your children within your walls, and leave not a stone on a stone within you, because you failed to recognize the time of your visitation."

Jesus was visiting his people—walking through the streets, proclaiming the kingdom of God, and healing his people. But they failed to recognize this moment of grace. A critical moment had arrived. God had sent his only Son. Many responded, but many more did not. Jesus said these words with tears running down his face—looking over the city he loved, looking over the people he loved—because they had refused to take the path to peace. Consequently, they faced God's judgment.

A time of visitation from God has a purpose: it is a time of mercy, but it also heralds a time of judgment. Jesus visited the city of Jerusalem, but the people of Jerusalem missed God's visitation to them.

The consequences of missing this hour of visitation were disastrous. Luke 19:45-46 tells us that Jesus immediately acted in such a way as to foreshadow the impending judgment on Jerusalem. He went into the temple and cleansed it by ejecting the traders, saying: "Scripture has it 'My house is meant for a house of prayer' but you have made it 'a den of thieves.'"

But this was only the beginning. Everything Jesus prophesied came to pass. The Jewish historian Josephus writes that a few years before 70 A.D. a man ran up and down the streets during a great Jewish festival crying, "Woe! Woe to the city! Woe to the people!" Shortly afterwards, a constellation appeared in the sky shaped in the form of a sword hanging over the city. Finally, on the feast of Passover in 70 A.D., on the thirty-seventh anniversary of the crucifixion of Jesus Christ, the Roman armies came. In the following months, thousands of Jews perished. Women and children were burned to death on the rooftop of the temple. Five hundred crosses were erected around the city on which to crucify those who resisted the Roman army. The temple was torn down and the city of Jerusalem was destroyed. Truly, a stone was not left standing on a stone. The Jewish nation was dispersed to the four corners of the earth. Everything that Jesus said would come to pass came to pass. The cleansing of the temple was a foreshadowing of God's purification of his people; the destruction of Jerusalem is a foreshadowing of the final judgment.

I believe that we are living right now in a time of visitation. I believe that God gives chances to individuals. I believe that God gives chances to cities. I believe that God gives chances to nations. I believe that God gives chances to generations. Today, God is giving us a chance. He is visiting us in an extraordinary way. For the first time since the early days of Christianity, we see the pouring out of the charismatic gifts of the Spirit, not just in special saints and holy people, but in a broad way throughout the body of Christ. We are witnessing in our century the raising up of mighty ministries of healing and preaching of the gospel. For the first time in history, the gospel is literally being proclaimed around the world, thanks to modern means of communication such as radio and television. Our generation is experiencing a visitation from God.

However, in this time, as in other times of visitation, we are faced with a choice. The choice is one of repentance or judgment. Unfortunately, many are choosing judgment. Jesus continues to weep over the cities of the world today because so many people who bear his name—who have been blessed with a Christian heritage—are repudiating their heritage. Many are openly hostile to God and to the one whom he has sent—Jesus Christ. We see in much of our world a rejection of God's word and his law that can only lead to a living hell on earth as human beings, caught up in the spirit of evil and lawlessness, unrestrainedly turn against one another and devour one another.

## The Condition of the World Today

What time is it? What time are we living in? What is happening in the generation that we are a part of? What are the signs of the times that the Lord wants us to recognize so that we can choose wisely how to spend our life?

A passage in Romans 1:18-32 provides us with a profound analysis of what we are experiencing in the world around us:

> The wrath of God is being revealed from heaven against the irreligious and perverse spirit of men, who, in this perversity of theirs, hinder the truth. In fact, whatever can be known about God is clear to them; he himself made it so. Since the creation of the world, invisible realities, God's eternal power and divinity, have become visible, recognized through the things he has made. Therefore these men are inexcusable. They certainly had knowledge of God, yet they did not glorify him as God or give him thanks; they stultified themselves through speculating to no purpose, and their senseless hearts were darkened. They claimed to be wise, but turned into fools instead; they exchanged the glory of the immortal God for images representing mortal man, birds, beasts, and snakes. In consequence, God delivered them up in their lusts to unclean practices; they engaged in the mutual degradation of their bodies, these men who exchange the truth of God for a lie and

worshipped and served the creature rather than the Creator—blessed be he forever, amen! God therefore delivered them up to disgraceful passions. Their women exchanged natural intercourse for unnatural, and the men gave up natural intercourse with women and burned with lust for one another. Men did shameful things with other men, and thus received in their own persons the penalty for their perversity. They did not see fit to acknowledge God, so God delivered them up to their own depraved sense to do what is unseemly. They are filled with every kind of wickedness: maliciousness, greed, ill will, envy, murder, bickering, deceit, craftiness. They are gossips and slanderers, they hate God, are insolent, haughty, boastful, ingenious in their wrongdoing and rebellious toward their parents. One sees in them men without conscience, without loyalty, without affection, without pity. They know God's just decree that all who do such things deserve death; yet they not only do them but approve them in others.

I believe we are living in a time when one thousand seven hundred years of Christian influence on Western civilization is being stripped away in our courts of law, in our educational systems, and in our culture and customs. We are living in a time of massive rebellion against God and against his word. We are reaping the whirlwind of acts of apostasy and rebellion sown deep into Western culture over the past several centuries and especially during the last twenty or thirty years. Things have been happening around us that most people never imagined would happen. During recent years, we have seen a vast outpouring of skepticism about the authority of God's word. Once again, the primordial temptation and rebellion against God is being repeated in our midst. Satan is repeating his primordial invitation by telling us, "You can be gods yourselves. You can be arbitrators of good and evil yourselves." Once again, men and women are responding to Satan's invitation. Once again, Satan is seducing many people into infidelity to God and his word.

Increasingly people are worshipping the creature instead of worshipping God. Increasingly they are putting their own desires before the needs of others. They are focusing on their own self-fulfillment and satisfying their own desires. This attitude is being fueled by multi-million dollar advertising campaigns that say, "Whatever you want, you deserve. Reach out and take it. "The voice of the serpent that rang out in the Garden of Eden is ringing in the ears of the human race today. "You will be like God. You will know what is good and evil. You will be gods yourselves." Many think they are wise thinking they know where fulfillment lies, but they are becoming fools instead. The consequence of rejecting God in order to worship the creature is enslavement to one's disordered desires.

We see the consequences of rejecting God in the society around us. Psychologists report that a growing number of people who come to them no longer have any control over their impulses. After being told for years to do their own thing, many are doing it. Many are killing, robbing, raping, committing adultery, and doing whatever else they please. They are living in a hell on earth under the terrifying reign of the evil one.

Furthermore, many are inviting people who bear the name of Christ to throw away their Christian heritage so that they will not "miss out" on what is happening in our culture. They encourage others to reach out for whatever they desire because they "deserve" it. They are telling others that there is no truth and that they are free to make their own rules. As a result, human life is disintegrating. We see this in the increasing growth of sexual perversity and the formation of organized power groups that aim to strip away any protection for God's people by introducing changes in our culture and in our laws that are contrary to God's word.

But sin never brings anything good. The glory that Satan promises is bitterly disappointing. We always experience in our own person the penalty for sin. We experience it in this life by the twisting and perverting of human life and the disintegration of the body, mind, and spirit; the penalty is experienced in the next life by eternal separation from God. God wants us to know that indeed "the wages of sin is death" (Rom 6:23). Sin does not bring happiness or wholeness; sin brings death, psychological disintegration, and physical decay.

In the passage from Romans quoted earlier, St. Paul says that one of the signs of rebellion against God is sexual confusion and disorder. Today it is becoming more and more apparent that the promises of the sexual revolution were lies and that the people who followed the false gospel of the sexual revolution are now paying the penalty. For example, 20,000,000 Americans today have herpes, a veneral disease for which there is no known cure. Within recent months, a growing number of people, primarily active homosexuals and drug users, have contracted a disease called Acquired Immune Deficiency Syndrome (AIDS) for which there is no cure and which appears to be fatal. These people are experiencing in their own bodies the penalty for their sin. But there is also some joint responsibility. An article in the September 9, 1983 issue of the *New England Journal of Medicine* has raised the possibility that AIDS may spread to some people who are not active homosexuals or drug users. If it does, we will experience as a society the penalty for exchanging the truth of God for a lie. For many years, people said that lifestyle is a matter of personal choice, an option with no societal consequences. Now our society is experiencing the penalty for believing this lie.

Proverbs 5:22-23 tells us, "By his own iniquities the wicked man will be caught, in the meshes of his own sin he will be held fast; He will die from lack of discipline, through the greatness of his folly he will be lost." The penalty might not be apparent the first day, the first week, or the first year. But the penalty will be paid. The wages of sin is death. The man or woman who turns from God literally risks death—now, in their own body, and later, in the life of the world to come.

The disintegration effects of sin are manifest in families as well as in personal lives. Dr. Armand Nicholi, a psychiatrist on the faculty of Harvard Medical School, has offered this chilling analysis of the current state of the family:

The trend toward quick and easy divorce and the ever increasing divorce rate subjects more and more children to physically and emotionally absent parents. The divorce rate has risen by 700 percent in this century and continues to rise. There is now one divorce for every 1.8 marriages. Over a million children a year are involved in divorce cases and 13 million children under eighteen have one or both parents missing... The family is also affected by the lack of impulse control in our culture today... The deep moral confusion we have observed over the past decade seems to have lifted all restraint. During the past ten years, I have noticed a marked change in the type of problems that bring people to a psychiatrist. Previously, a great many came because of their inability to express impulses and feelings. Today, the majority come because of an inability to *control* their impulses. (People in my field relate this lack of control to the declining influence of the father in the home.)

Aggression in the home has been increasing steadily. . . Even more prevalent in society is the failure to control sexual impulses. The number of illegitimate births in this country continues to rise. . . . A home in which both parents are available to the child emotionally has become the exception rather than the rule.

What about the future, asks Dr. Nicholi, if these trends continue?

First, the quality of family life will continue to deteriorate, producing a society with a higher incidence of mental illness than ever before. Ninty-five percent of our hospital beds may be taken up by mentally ill patients. This illness will be characterized primarily by a lack of self-control. We can expect the assassination of people in authority to be a frequent occurrence, as well as events like the sixteen-year-old girl who recently began shooting people "for the fun of it."

Crimes of violence will increase, even those within the family. . . The suicide rate will continue to rise. . . In the past twenty years, however, the suicide rate in ten to fourteen-year-olds has tripled. We already are producing an enormous number of angry, depressed, and suicidal kids. (Quotes from *Christianity Today,* May 25, 1979.)

Not only can individuals experience the bitter disintegration that follows in the wake of sin, not only can families experience such disintegration, but whole societies, cultures, and nations can drift into profoundly evil patterns and experience the awful consequences. It has happened before and it can happen again.

The example of what happened in Nazi Germany is well known; less well known are the striking parallels to what is happening in our own society today.

The corruption of influential segments of the intellectual and medical elite was a significant factor in paving the way for the massive slaughter of the Jews. One individual who was particularly instrumental in this was H.S. Chamberlain, whose racial theories laid the foundation for Nazi policies. William Shirer, in his book *The Rise and Fall of the Third Reich,* describes Chamberlain and his work:

Hypersensitive and neurotic and subject to frequent nervous breakdowns, Chamberlain was given to seeing demons who, by own account, drove him on relentlessly to seek new fields of study and get on with his prodigious writings. . . Once in 1898, when he was returning from Italy, the presence of a demon became so forceful that he got off the train at Gardone, shut himself up in a hotel room for eight days, and, abandoning some work on music that he had contemplated, wrote feverishly on a biological thesis until he had the germ of the theme that would dominate all of his later works: race and history. . . Since he felt himself goaded on by demons, his books (on Wagner, Goethe, Kant, Christianity and race) were written in the grip of a terrible fever, a veritable trance, a state of self-induced intoxication, so that, as he says in his autobiography, *Lebenswegt,* he was often unable to recognize them as his own work, because they surpassed his expectations.

Many of the "best and the brightest" perpetrated the holocaust or closed their eyes to it. Robert Lifton, a Yale University psychiatrist, has noted that German physicians, "heirs to Europe's proudest medical tradition," participated in the mass slaughter and grisly human experiments in the Nazi death camps:

Doctors were the embodiment of Nazi political and racial ideology in its ultimate murderous form. The killing came to be projected as a medical operation. . . If you have a gangrenous growth, you have to remove it. . . If you view the

Jews as death-tainted, then killing them seems to serve life. . . *Most killing is not done out of sadism, not even most Nazi killing. . . The murders are done out of a perverted vision of life enhancement."* (*Time* magazine, June 25, 1979, European edition. Emphasis added.)

In Western society today, are not many of the "best and brightest" participating in and justifying the slaughter of millions of babies in their mother's wombs? Is not the slaughter being done, as the slaughter of the Jews was done, to supposedly "enhance the quality of life"? We say it can't happen here. Isn't it happening already? Is not abortion rightly called the silent holocaust, on a scale even greater than the destruction of six million Jews in Nazi Germany?

The tragic reality of Satanically inspired deception and moral and spiritual blindness affecting the fabric of a whole society, as well as individuals and families, cannot be overlooked.

### A Time of Repentance or Judgment

Pope John Paul II has said that there are two kinds of evangelism going on in the world today. One is evangelism for the kingdom of God. The other is evangelism for the kingdom of darkness. One is evangelism for love; the other is evangelism for lust, greed, bitterness, resentment, and jealousy.

A struggle is underway between the gospel and the anti-gospel. On one side are the servants of

Jesus Christ who proclaim salvation and try to draw men into the kingdom of God. On the other side are those who have become victims of Satan— who have themselves been touched by darkness or who are in bondage to their own passions. They are encouraging others to follow them on the path that leads to destruction. Thirty years ago, social pressure in this country encouraged fidelity to God's word. Today, social pressure encourages infidelity to God's word. The world tells us, "Seek yourself and you'll find yourself." Mark 8:35 tells us that if we seek Jesus Christ we will find ourselves: "Whoever would preserve his life will lose it, but whoever loses his life for my sake and the gospel's will preserve it."

When Jesus' disciples asked what they would get out of following him, Jesus assured them that they would receive much in this life as well as eternal life in the world to come. It is better to experience times of loneliness here on earth than to try to assuage that loneliness by entering into unrighteous relationships for a short time now. It is better to live a life of poverty here on earth than to live a life of wealth that was gained through unrighteous means. It is better to be lonely and poor now if the alternative means we will lose eternal life.

We are not living in a neutral time. We are in the midst of spiritual warfare. We are not simply dealing with well-meaning people who are unwittingly mistaken. Rather, I believe, as St. Paul says, that we are locked in spiritual combat with powers and principalities. A ferocious war is being waged under the surface of our society. Satan, like a roaring lion, is seeking those he might devour. He is using every falsehood, evil power, and false device at his disposal to seduce the people of God. God is calling his people to recognize that war has been declared, that a struggle is going on for the destiny of the human race. You and I have been caught up in that struggle. We have been touched by the spirit of God and called by the person of Christ to take our stand. How important it is that we hear God's word and respond to it! How important it is that we root our lives in the truth of God's word and prefer it to anything. Jesus said, "I am **the** way, I am **the** truth, I am **the** life; no one comes to the Father except through me" (Jn 14:6). Jesus did not say, "I am an option. I am a choice. I am a truth." Jesus said, "I am **the** way, **the** truth, and **the** life; no one comes to the Father except through me." In 2 Thessalonians 2:6-7, St. Paul says that at the end of time there will be an unleashing of the power of evil and a period of unrestrained lawlessness. A "restrainer" that was holding back the work of Satan will be removed: "You know what restrains him until he shall be revealed in his own time. The secret force of lawlessness is already at work, mind you, but there is one who holds him back until that restrainer shall be taken from the scene."

I believe that over the past twenty years, we have seen in our society an accelerating removal of all kinds of restraints on evil. In fact, our society flaunts evil! People are doing and saying blasphemous things in public and openly declaring their hatred of God. In Revelation 6:10, the souls of those who had been martyred because of the witness they bore to the word of God cried out at the top of their voices, "How long will it be . . . before you judge our cause and avenge our blood among the inhabitants of the earth?" I believe that the souls of those millions slaughtered by abortion and through infanticide in our day, as well as the Christian martyrs of our day, are now crying out to God for justice. Their outcry is reaching the throne of God, as it did in the days of Sodom and Gomorrah. In Romans 12:19, St. Paul tells us that God says, "Vengeance is mine; I will repay." I believe that God is saying the same thing to our generation today: "Vengeance is mine; I will repay." God will not be mocked forever. The Creator will reclaim his creation through fire—the fire of his love that invites us to purification and repentance and the fire of his judgment that punishes those who persist in rebellion.

I believe that time is now running out for our generation. I believe that our generation will see the fire of God. Our generation faces a choice: repentance or judgment. Time ran out for Sodom and Gomorrah. Time ran out for the generation of Noah. Time tragically ran out for the city of Jerusalem. And time is running out for us.

I believe that God gives warnings to his people to turn back to him before it is too late. God warned the city of Jerusalem before the Roman armies destroyed it. He warned Nineveh and he warned Noah's generation. Jesus indicates in Luke 13:1-5 that God also gives his people warnings by means of "natural disasters." He pointed out that the eighteen people who were killed by a falling tower in Siloam were no more guilty of sin than anyone else who lived in Jerusalem, and he warned his listeners to take heed and repent before it was too late for them.

I believe that God is giving us warnings today to turn back to him before it is too late. His heralds and messengers of the gospel alert people to the truth of Christianity. Furthermore, I believe that God is giving us signs and warnings that even the most secularized people can understand. The various kinds of incurable veneral diseases, such as herpes and AIDS, are obvious signs that the way of sexual immorality is a way of death, manifesting that the promises of the "sexual revolution" were lies. The strange weather of recent years—from droughts in Australia and Africa to floods in California and Louisiana, with earthquakes and volcanoes in between—may be yet other signs that God is sending us to convince us to take heed and repent before it is too late, to draw our attention back to his sovereignty and to recognize that human life is fragile and dependent on his power. And is not a sword hanging over the heads of all of us today—the sword of nuclear destruction? We are all targeted many times over. I believe it is not only arms control negotiations that will determine whether nuclear weapons are used or not, but the intercession, prayer, repentance, and evangelism of God's people has an important role to play.

A time of visitation is a time of choice. Will it be

repentance or judgment? God expects a response. Jesus wept over Jerusalem because the people did not respond. I believe that Jesus is weeping over many cities in the world today because they are missing this hour of his visitation. What a responsibility this gives those of us who hear this message and know the person of Jesus Christ! We are to be his witnesses in this time of visitation, heralds of his gospel, intercessors for our family, friends, neighbors, and fellow citizens, asking God to have mercy and to turn our hearts to repentance.

## The Choice We Face

This is a time of crisis for the church and the world. There is only one thing to do: turn to Jesus Christ and do whatever he tells us to do.

For some time now, I have had the following verse from Isaiah 55:6 in my heart: "Seek the Lord while he may be found, call him while he is near." This word came at a time in the history of Israel when the word of God was plentiful and abundant. I believe we are living in another such time. I believe that the Lord is giving us today a word that he wants us to share with our friends, relatives, neighbors, and co-workers. I feel that this word is precisely, "Seek the Lord while he may be found, call him while he is near."

How do we seek God? To seek God means to turn towards him, but every act of turning towards necessarily involves a turning away: in this case, a turning away from lukewarmness, from trying to serve two masters, from trying to keep one foot in both camps until we see who is going to win. In short, seeking God means turning away from the broad and easy way that most people are taking and setting out on the narrow path that leads to eternal life. Jesus tells us, "Enter through the narrow gate. The gate that leads to damnation is wide, the road is clear, and many choose to travel it. But how narrow is the gate that leads to life, how rough the road, and how few there are who find it!" (Mt 7:13-14) We will not enter the kingdom of God by drifting along the easy way that everyone is taking. We can enter the kingdom only if we are obedient to his person, his word, his will, and his Spirit. We have to turn away from sin and turn toward him.

I believe that the destiny of our generation is hanging right now in the balance. We are faced with a choice: repentance or judgment. We who have been touched by this visitation have a critical role to play. Our intercessory prayer, like Abraham's prayer for Sodom and Gommorah and Jonah's ministry to Niniveh, is important and valuable in resisting the tide of evil that is flooding our homes and our cities. Today, God is inviting us once again to build an ark—an ark formed by our relationships with him and with one another. He wants us to invite everyone whom we know and who is willing to enter into these relationships. The destiny of our generation is hanging in the balance. God is preparing an ark for those who are willing to follow him. And the waters are rising.

St. Paul warns us: "Do not deceive yourselves: no fornicators, idolators, or adulterers, no sodomites, thieves, misers, or drunkards, no slanderers or robbers will inherit God's kingdom"(1 Cor 6: 9-10). We all have a tendency to deceive ourselves into thinking that we can make a compromise here and there. But we should not delude ourselves with the idea that there are no requirements for entering God's kingdom. We should not delude ourselves with the notion that everyone will be saved no matter what kind of life they live. In this time of visitation we are faced with a choice. In a very real way, Christians today are standing with one foot on the dock and one foot in the boat—while the two move apart. Our society and the gospel are increasingly moving apart. Christians today have to evaluate their lives in light of God's word and choose to avoid those things that sap their zeal for Christ. It may be a certain magazine, a certain television program, a certain fashion, or a certain friend. There are certain magazines we should not read and certain television programs we should not watch if we want to remain pure and holy for Jesus Christ. Often we should not wear certain fashions that our smart and sophisticated neighbors are wearing if we want to live a life of godliness for Jesus Christ. And often we should not cultivate friendships with certain people if we want to remain faithful to Jesus Christ.

Life is short. Sometimes—after a sleepless night or a tiresome day—life might seem very long. But in the perspective of eternity, life is short. As the psalmist says, "Man's days are like those of grass; like a flower of the field he blooms; the wind sweeps over him and he is gone, and his place knows him no more" (Ps 103:15-16). Only one thing is necessary as we live our short lives: to seek the Lord while he may be found and to hear and obey his voice while he is speaking to us. We really make only one significant decision in our lives—the decision to be either for or against Jesus Christ. We have to decide to lay down the weapons of our rebellion and acknowledge that Jesus Christ is the rightful ruler of the universe, the rightful ruler of each and every one of us. We have to decide that we want to become part of his kingdom and be counted among his friends.

What does it mean to be Jesus' friends? In Luke 10:38-42, we read about Jesus' visit to his friends—Martha, Mary, and Lazarus. Martha was trying to serve the Lord by cooking the meal while Mary sat at Jesus' feet and listened to him. Martha complained that Mary was not helping her. Jesus said, "Martha, Martha, you are anxious and upset about many things." They were good things to be concerned about, but Jesus went on to say, "One thing only is required. Mary has chosen the better portion and she shall not be deprived of it." In other words, Mary chose to listen to what Jesus had to say. Jesus' word to us is all-important. Jesus himself tells us, "The heavens and the earth will pass away but my words will not pass"(Mk 13:31). We need to trust the word of God more than we trust the ground on which we stand. The ground may crumble. Heaven and earth will pass away. But every part of God's word will be fulfilled. We can trust the word of God with all our heart. We can rest the weight of our life on that word and not be disappointed.

We live in a time of crisis. In a time of crisis, we need to turn to Jesus and do whatever he tells us. I believe that one of the main things he is telling us right now is to seek him while there is time and to call upon him while he is near. Time is short. Important things are hanging in the balance.

Who do we seek? Who do we call upon? Who do we place our trust in? No one else but he through whom everything that is was created:

He is the image of the invisible God, the first-born of all creatures. In him everything in heaven and on earth was created, things visible and invisible, whether thrones or dominations, principalities or powers; all were created through him, and for him. He is before all else that is. In him everything continues in being. It is he who is the head of the body, the church; he who is the beginning, the first-born of the dead, so that primacy may be his in everything. It pleased God to make absolute fullness reside in him and, by means of him, to reconcile everything in his person, both on earth and in the heavens, making peace through the blood of his cross. (Col 1:15-20)

Not only was everything created through him, but everything was created for him. Everything that is finds its meaning and fulfillment only insofar as it comes under his reign and rule. That is the reason why the only way to be fully human is to be in Jesus Christ—to be a Christian.

The human race was created for the Son of God. We have come forth from his hand. We are structured in such a way that our lives will work well only when we are in union with him. Everything that our fallen world needs has been provided through the sacrifice of Jesus Christ on the cross. One drop of his blood was enough to take away the sins of the entire world.

He whom we seek is Creator and Lord. He whom we call upon is the Lamb slain for our sins. He whom we draw close to is the one who longed to gather us together as a mother hen gathers her chicks. He whom we breathe and live in is the one who weeps over our cities and offers us the path to peace by showing us how to avoid judgment and catastrophe.

I once spoke to a Christian businessman, the head of a very large company, who had spent most of his life serving the Lord's work as a dedicated Christian layman. He told me that for several months he had been waking up at night asking himself, "Am I really using my time in a way that I will not profoundly regret when I stand before the Lord?" He thought the Lord was speaking to him through these incidents. I think the Lord wants us to ask ourselves that very same question: are we spending our time in way that we will not pro-foundly regret when we stand before the Lord? Picture yourself standing before the Lord. Ask yourself: "What will seem important? What will not seem important? What will I regret? What will I not regret?" God will give you wisdom and light as you ask yourself these questions. He might show you some adjustments to make in your life right now.

What is really important in the short time that God has given us? It is to "love the Lord our God with your whole heart, with your whole soul, and with all your mind" (Mt 22:37). It is to "love your neighbor as yourself" (Mt 22:39). This means we must confess our sin, be forgiven, and be recon-ciled with God. I believe it is also of utmost impor-tance to help others make the same choice and decision for God in the short time God has given them. I believe that the Lord wants us more and more to look at life as he looks at it—in the light of eternity. In that light, life is very short indeed. The Lord is calling us to be witnesses in a time of visitation—witnesses in the Church and witnesses in the world. We are called to be witnesses to the person of Jesus and witnesses to the Christian way of life despite the humiliation and mockery that Christians meet in today's society. We are called to intercede for our family and friends, neighbors and co-workers, so that God might have mercy on them and give them the grace they need to respond to him. How much God is willing to do for those who are his friends! How much he will do through his friends' intercession, their evangelism, their resistance to evil, and their love and generosity! As we live that way, we will be more and more able to fervently pray as the prayer of our hearts, "Come, Lord Jesus, come!".

**Ralph Martin** heads a teaching, writing, and speaking ministry in Ann Arbor, Michigan. To receive his periodic newsletter, write to Renewal Ministries, Box 7712, Ann Arbor, Michigan 48107.